Python Programming

The Crash Course To Learn How To Master Python Coding Language With PRACTICAL Exercises To APPLY Theory And Some TIPS And TRICKS To Learn Faster Computer Programming

JOSEPH MINING

I0510423

form the information ultimately takes. This includes copied versions of the work, both physical, digital, and audio unless express consent of the Publisher is provided beforehand.

The only exception is for the inclusion of brief quotations in a review. Any additional rights reserved.

Furthermore, the information that can be found within the pages described forthwith shall be considered both accurate and truthful when recounting facts. As such, any use, correct or incorrect, of the provided information will render the Publisher free of responsibility as to the actions taken outside of their direct purview. Regardless, there are zero scenarios where the original author or the Publisher can be deemed liable in any fashion for any damages or hardships that may result from any of the information discussed herein.

Additionally, the information in the following pages is intended only for
informational purposes, and should thus be thought of as universal. As befitting its nature, it is presented without assurance regarding its prolonged validity or interim quality. Mentioned trademarks are done without written consent, and can in no way be considered an endorsement from the trademark holder.

Table of Contents

Introduction

The following chapters will discuss everything that you need to know to get started with the Python coding language. There are different coding languages that you can work with. Some of them are going to be easier to work with, and some are harder and are only recommended if you are someone who codes regularly. However, when it comes to the Python coding language, even someone who has never done a bit of coding in their lives can benefit and learn all about it.

This guidebook is going to dive right into a lot of the neat things that you can do with the Python language. Whether you just want to learn a bit more about coding, enhance some of the skills that are needed in other coding languages and add to your portfolio, or have some neat ideas for an application or program that you would like to develop, the Python coding language is a great option for you to get started with.

This guidebook is going to start with some information on what Python is all about, as well as why so many computer programmers like to choose this as their coding language. We will explore some of the benefits such as: why it is so powerful yet easy for a beginner to work with, how to install it on your system, no matter what kind of operating system you are working with. Also, some of the basic parts of the code that you should know to help you develop on some of the harder stuff later on.

The rest of this guidebook is going to focus on all of the cool things that you can implement into your codes, no matter what program you would like to develop. Some of the different topics that we are going to explore when dealing with Python coding language will include the loops, conditional statements, regular expressions, how to raise an exception, and so much more!

There are so many amazing things you can do with Python language. Even as a beginner, you are going to be impressed by how easy it is to learn this language and yet be amazed at the amount of power that comes behind all of your codes. When you are ready to learn more about the Python language, and how to use the different aspects of your codes, make sure to check out this guidebook to help you get started.

There are many books on this subject on the market—thanks again for choosing this one! Every effort was made to ensure it is full of as much useful information as possible. Please enjoy!

Chapter 1: What Is the Python Coding Language, and Why Is It So Beneficial?

There are a lot of different coding languages out there that you can work with. Each of them is going to have their benefits and a lot of neat features that come with it. But when it comes to a coding language that is easy to use, that is great for beginners, easy-to-read, lots of options, open-sourced, and still has a lot of power that comes behind it, then the Python coding language is one of the best options out there.

The Python coding language has been a favorite for a lot of people over the years. They enjoy the fact that they can learn this language and still make some fantastic codes in progress, even though they are beginners and may not have worked with this coding in the past—or any coding, for that matter.

Python is a computer user's programming language. Even as a beginner, you can learn this language quickly, but there is still a lot of power behind it, which allows you to do the codes that you want. You can make complex commercial applications, automating some housekeeping tasks for your system, or have some fun and make your games and programs.

Of course, just like with all the other programming languages, Python has a set of rules and structures that all programs need to follow. No matter what code you decide to write, it is important that you follow the rules in Python. However, compared to some of the other programming languages that are out there, you will find that this coding language is simple, compact, and very powerful. As a beginner, you will catch on quickly, and can write some of your codes in no time!

In the past, a lot of people were worried about learning a coding language. They were worried that these languages were too tough to learn, that they would get frustrated, and that only those who had spent their whole lives around computers could even attempt to write their codes—and maybe with some of the older codes, this was true.

Thanks to a lot of the newer codes introduced recently, the idea that only those gifted in computer programming could code has faded away. With many of the codes that are coming out now, including Python, anyone can learn a few of the syntaxes for what they want to do, or even find some premade codes online and make some changes. And since many of these codes are open-sourced, it is easier than ever to learn how to use them and develop the codes to meet your needs.

The modern coding languages are much better than what was found in the past with most coding languages. Gone are the days that even professionals struggled to keep bugs out of the system—and now is the time for anyone to learn how to use a coding language for their needs. This is all thanks to the development of many great object-oriented programming languages like Python.

Many coding and programming languages are available for you to choose from based on the programs and applications that you would like to create. But even with all of those different options that you have available, it is common for many computer programmers, whether they are beginners or have worked with coding in the past to choose the Python coding language.

There are a lot of reasons why people like to work with the Python code, rather than some of the other options out there. Some of the most common reasons for going with the Python language include:

There are a lot of libraries that provide you with the support you need. Just a glance through the Python environment is going to show you that many extensions and libraries will provide you with all of the help that you need to get started. You can find the classes, objects, and functions inside the language to make it easier to create all of the codes that you need. Also, it is possible to bring in some of the third party libraries from outside sources to the mix to help you get more of the features and power that you want.

Features of integration: Python is a great language to work with for many reasons, but one of these is because it can integrate with the Enterprise Application Integration. This means that you can work with some of the different Python components that it has, including COM and COBRA. There are also some control capabilities so that it can work with C, Java, and C++. It can work with many markup languages, including XML, and can use any of the modern operating systems so it will work with whatever you have when you get started.

Allows the programmer to be more productive. The Python language has a ton of different designs that are going to work here, object orientation in it, and the support libraries that you need. Thanks to all of these various resources, and the fact that it is super easy to work on this program, it is easy for the programmer to find ways to increase how productive they are. They can use this kind of productivity to help them with some of the other coding languages you want to work with as well.

It is easy to learn: The primary purpose behind this language is that it was developed to be easy to use and easy to adapt to different purposes. This makes it easy for a programmer to work with, even if they are a beginner. We are going to learn more about this language and look at some of the codes that go with Python and help you to get the most out of this language so that, even as a beginner, you can write some powerful programs.

It is easy to read through this language. As you look through some of the codes that come in this language, you will find that it is pretty easy to read through the codes, even before learning what they mean. There isn't a lot of unnecessary information that has to show up in the code, and it is all in English, so it is easy to understand the words found in it.

Python can provide you with a lot of programming power. One thing that you may be impressed with when you start on the Python language is the amount of power that is behind it. Even though this language is classified as more of a beginners' language, it is easy to adapt it and learn how to use it for any program and application. And if you learn how to combine it with some of the other high-end coding languages out there, you will see it come with even more power as well.

A big community of support Since Python is one of the biggest and most popular of all the coding languages worldwide; it has a big community of those who are learning how to use the language and those who are already well-versed in how to use it. You can take advantage of all this information and learn from it. You can ask questions, watch tutorials, or find out something new with this language as you go.

It is an open-sourced program. What this means is that you will be able to get the code for free, as well as any updates that come with it. There are some third-party add-ons that you will need to pay for if you choose to use them, but it is possible to use Python without those so you will get it all for free.

As you can see, there are a lot of great things that you are going to enjoy when you decide to get started with the Python code and use it for your own needs. Whether you are trying to add a new programming language to your arsenal to help you work well with your codes, or you are a beginner who wants to enter into the world of technology, the Python coding language is one of the best options for you to get started with.

Getting Python on Your System

Before you can utilize the information in this guidebook and write out any codes to help you develop your programs, you need first to make sure that Python is on your computer or the other system that you are using. And if it isn't there, then we need to pick out a version of Python and then download it.

Depending on your computer system, it is possible that you already have it available on your computer. Check to see if this is true. If you find that your system doesn't have this language on it, or you are not happy with the Python version that is already present on your computer, then it is time to either add it on or make the changes to a newer version.

Since Python is an open-sourced programming language, you can get everything that you need for free. If you want to add something special to the environment, or you want to have a different library, you may have to go through and add that on and pay for it. But if you want to use the basics of the Python language, as well as the great libraries and other resources with it, then you can get it for free.

With that said, there are going to be a few different available versions of Python, and choosing the one that you would like to work with the most can be a bit tricky. Since Python is going to be an interpreted language, it comes with a lot of advantages over some of the other coding languages that are out there. You will notice that one of the advantages over the others is that Python can grow and make the changes that are necessary for your computing needs. Like the applications that you can find on your computer, Python is always being developed, and these new features that come with that development can refine and change Python throughout time.

Since Python has been around for several years now, there are a few different versions of Python that have been released through that time. All of the versions have been accepted widely, but they are going to provide you with some different benefits and features over the old version. Some of the options that are available for a programmer to choose from when trying to pick a version of this coding language to work with include:

Python 2.X: There are several versions of Python 2 that you can choose from. This is one of the older versions on the market, and while it still works fine if it is the version found on your computer, it is becoming a bit dated, and many people are going to work with one of the newer Python 3 options.

Python 3: If you can choose a version to go with, then Python 3 is going to be the best option. It is the latest and includes most of the third party add-ons that you will need, the developments and features that you need for most projects, and it is going to have updates that come out. If you are choosing to download a version of Python onto your computer, then this is the best one to go with.

Installing the Interpreter on Python

Now, before you can write out any of the codes that we want to explore in this guidebook, or use the Python language at all, it is important you go through and install the interpreter. Installing this language is going to depend on the operating system that you would like to use to run this, as well as the source where you are getting the installation. There are a few different sources for downloading this language, and some are going to be more of a modified version of the code rather than the original release, so make sure that you are checking into this ahead of time as well.

From here, we are going to break up this whole process of installation and see how it behaves on the different operating systems. This makes it easier for you to get the Python language downloaded on the system that you need without any problems.

Mac OS X

The first operating system that we are going to work with is for those who are using the Mac computer. If you have this operating system, then you will find that Python 2 is going to be installed already on the computer. The exact version that comes with this will depend on the version of the operating system that you have running, and you can determine this quickly. Open up the app for the terminal and then type in the prompt: `python - V`

When you do this, the system is going to tell you what version of Python is already on here for you to use. If you are fine with using Python 2, then close out of that and move on to writing some of your codes. But it is also possible for you to install the

Python 3 version onto the computer. To check for this installation, you need to open that terminal app again, and then use the prompt "python3 -V" to help you get started.

By the default, Mac computers, and operating systems are not going to have this version of Python installed on them. If you would like to use this still, you will need to visit the python.org website and install a few of the options that are on there. This is often the best place to do your installation because it will make sure everything is added to your computer. So, once the download is done, you can open up Python and start writing the code. It is much better to have the interpreter, development tools, the IDLE, and the shell for Python already on your computer, rather than having to double check all the time and download things on their own.

Whether or not you can run the shell and the IDLE on Python are going to depend on the version that you will run on the computer, and your preferences on the matter. The commands that you can use that will bring up the applications for IDLE and the shell will include:

Type in "Idle" if you are working with a version of Python 2.
Type in "Idle3" if you are working with a version of Python 3.

Windows Systems

It is possible that you are going to want to work with the Python coding language on your Windows computer. You will not have the language automatically added to your computer because Microsoft already has its programming language present there. Python may not be standard here, but you can still go through and install it on the computer if you would like. You will also need to go through and add in the environment variables that you want because these are not done by default either. You will then be able to run any of the scripts that you need for Python going from the command prompt. The steps to get this done will include:

To set this up, you need to visit the official Python download page and grab the Windows installer. You can choose to do the latest version of Python 3, or go with another option. By default, the installer is going to provide you with the 32-bit version of Python, but you can choose to switch this to the 64-bit version if you wish. The 32-bit is often best to make sure that there aren't any compatibility issues with the older packages, but you can experiment if you wish.

Now, right click on the installer and select "Run as Administrator." There are going to be two options to choose from. You will want to pick out "Customize Installation."

On the following screen, make sure all of the boxes under "Optional Features" are clicked and then click to move on.

While under Advanced Options," you should pick out the location where you want Python to be installed. Click on Install. Give it some time to finish, and then close the installer.

Next, set the PATH variable for the system so that it includes directories that will consist of packages and other components that you will need later. To do this, use the following instructions:

Open up the Control Panel. Do this by clicking on the taskbar and typing in Control Panel. Click on the icon.

Inside the Control Panel, search for Environment. Then click on Edit the System Environment Variables. From here, you can click on the button for Environment Variables.

Go to the section for User Variables. You can either edit the PATH variable that is there or create one.

If there isn't a variable for PATH on the system, then create one by clicking on New. Make a name for the PATH variable, and add in the directories that you want. Click on close all the control Panel dialogs and move on.

Now, you can open up your command prompt. Do this by clicking on Start Menu, then Windows System, and then Command Prompt. Type in "`python`." This is going to load up the Python interpreter for you.

When you get to this point, the program is going to be all set up and easy to use on the Windows system. You can open up the interpreter when you are ready, as well as everything else that is needed and can work on writing out codes and creating the programs that you would like.

Linux System

And the final step that we will need to follow to get this coding language and all of its environment set up on your computer is to look at the steps that you can take for this on a Linux computer. As more and more computer programmers are moving to use the Linux system to help them get their work done and work with coding. It is always a good idea to learn how to make this work on this kind of operating system as well.

The very first step that we need to take is to check and see which version of Python is already on the system and check if Python 3 is already there. To check on this, you need to open up the command prompt on your computer and work with the following code inside:

```
$ python3 - - version
```

If you are on Ubuntu 16.10 or newer, then it is a simple process to install Python 3.6. You need to use the following commands:

```
$ sudo apt-get update
$ sudo apt-get install Python3.6
```

If you are relying on an older version or Ubuntu or another version, then you may want to work with the *deadsnakes* PPA, or another tool to help you download the Python 3.6 version. The code to do this includes:

```
$ sudo apt-get install software-properties-common
$ sudo add-apt repository ppa:deadsnakes/ppa
# sudo apt-get update
$ sudo apt-get install python3.6
```

One thing that you may note here is that if you are working with some of the other distributions that are available through this operating system, it is very likely that the whole program of Python 3 will be found on the system already. If not, you can use the package manager of the system to help. If you notice that the version of Python 3 is not the right one or not recent enough, for your needs, you can then use the same steps to make sure that a newer version of Python gets installed the way that you would like.

Working with the Python Interpreter

If you go through and do the standard installation through the Python program through python.org, then the work is going to be done for you here. It is going to contain all of the licensing and information and documentation that you need, along with the three files that are imperative to helping you develop and run all of the scripts that you need on system. These three files are going to include the shell, interpreter, and IDLE for Python.

First, we need to take a look at the interpreter. This is an important piece to the puzzle that you need to have in place because it is the part that will execute any of the scripts that you want to write in this language. The interpreter is then able to convert the .py script files into instructions, and can then go through and process them based on the file type and the code type that you decide to write in there.

Next, you are going to notice the IDLE of this language. IDLE is going to stand for the integrated development and learning environment. It will have all of the tools that you need to help develop programs in Python. You will find many tools in here including those for debugging, for the text editor, and the shell of the language.

Depending on which version you choose to go with on Python, you may find that the IDLE is either pretty basic or extensive and full. If you are looking through the IDLE that comes with Python, and you don't care for it, or you have done some research and have found a different version of the IDLE that you would like to work on better, you can download that in as well. Often, most people are okay with the IDLE, but they will choose to go with a different text editor to get more of the features that they want. But you can certainly stick with the text editor and IDLE that are present with Python and make some fantastic codes and programs in the process.

And finally, we are to the Python Shell. This is an important thing that you need to make sure gets downloaded on your computer because it is the interface that is part of the command line and very interactive, which works with the interpreter. This is the part that will hold onto any of the codes and the commands that you write out. If the shell can look at what you are writing and understands it, then it can execute the code, and the information that you want will show up on the screen. However, if you don't write the code correctly, or the shell isn't working correctly, then there are going to be problems with the code doing what you want.

All three of these components, as well as any of the other features that you need for your programming, can be essential to ensure that you can get the most out of writing your code. If you decide to go through python.org to download this information on any of your operating systems, then all three of those components are going to be downloaded and installed for you, making the work easier, and letting you get to work writing your codes in no time.

There are times, though, when the individual will choose to go outside of the python.org to get the version of Python that they want. This is fine if you decide to do that, but you do need to double-check the files that you are getting and see if those three main components are present in there or not. If they aren't, then make sure that you find each of them and that you will get them installed on your computer as well. Forgetting to do this, or just deciding not to, is going to guarantee that your codes are not going to work the way you want. So, you may as well get them done now rather than being frustrated later on.

Chapter 2: The Basics You Need to Know About the Python Code

Now that we have taken the time to learn a bit more about Python learning and all of the neat things that you can do with it, it is time to look a bit more in depth when it comes to the different parts that are available with Python. There are a lot of necessary parts that are going to show up in almost every code that you decide to write. You will notice that there are keywords that tell the program how to run. You will see that there are functions and identifiers, and a lot of other parts of the code that are super important.

As a beginner, it is a good idea to get a handle on these different parts so that you can get the best results overall. These will make it easier to work with some of the other parts that we talk about, and will ensure you can write out codes that suit your needs. Some of the basics that show up in the Python codes you will write include:

The Keywords

The first thing that we need to look at here is the keywords. These seem pretty simple, but it is so important to understand that they tell the compiler how it needs to act and behave with the projects that you are doing. These keywords are ones that are reserved to tell the compiler what it needs to do. Since they are reserved, the computer programmer needs to remember to use them properly so that the compiler can take that command and get things done.

You need only to use them in the specified parts of the code, or it leads to error messages and other problems. If you properly use them, the compiler will be given command of what you want it to do, and it can then execute the code in the right way. These words are essential to the whole code, and learning what they are is going to make code writing easier as well. You will be able to notice a lot of these keywords as we progress through this guidebook and write some of our codes.

The Importance of the Identifiers

The next thing that you need to learn about when you are writing your codes is the identifiers. These identifiers are going to come in handy when you are writing out codes in Python, and there are a number of these that you can work with. You will find that they do have a few names to them, and you may see them through this guidebook as variables, functions, classes, and functions—to name a few.

The good news here is that even though all of them have different names attached to them, and work in different ways in the code, they are still going to have the same rules when it is time to label and name them. This can make it a lot easier to remember the rules, ensuring that you do it correctly and that the information can be called out when the code needs it the most.

So, when naming these identifiers, the first rule that you have to keep in mind is how to name these. There are a lot of options that you can work with when it is time to name one of these identifiers. For example, you can use the underscore symbol, any number, and both lowercase and uppercase letters to get this all done. You can do any combination of this that you would like to name the identifier that you are using properly.

However, you have to remember that there is an order that needs to happen with these, or they are not going to react the way that you would like. First, you are not able to start the name of this identifier with a number. You also do not want to leave any spaces if you are using more than one word to name the identifier. So, you cannot write out the name of an identifier as "3 kids" or "three kids," but you could do "threekids" or "three_kids," and it would save right. If you try to go against any of these rules, you will see that the compiler will bring up an error signal for you.

When you are trying to pick out the name that you would like to give your identifier, you can easily pick from the rules above and also remember that you need to pick out a name that you can remember that makes sense for that part of the code. If you are writing out the code and you named an identifier something that you cannot remember or difficult, then you will run into trouble adding it in later on. But outside of those few rules, you can give your identifier any name that you would like.

Working with the Control Flow

Another topic that we need to explore when we are working in the Python language is known as the control flow. This is important because it has been set up in a way to make sure that all codes you write in Python are going to be done in the right way, and that the compiler will be able to read them.

There are a few strings that you may try to use in the code, and you need to make sure that all of the parts are in the right place at the right time, or the compiler is going to run into trouble reading them. The good news is that the control flow in Python is going to be pretty easy to work with, and you can catch on to some of the rules, and how they work in Python by glancing through a few of the codes that are present throughout this guidebook.

The Statements

Statements are a pretty easy thing to catch, but we are going to take a moment to bring them up and help you understand the best way to work with them. When we are talking about statements in this language, we are talking about the string of code that the computer programmer is going to write out, and then have the compiler list it out on the computer screen.

Any time that you tell the compiler a set of instructions that you would like to work on, you will find that these are going to be the statements that you are working on in the code as well. As long as these statements are written out in the right way, the compiler is going to read them, and then give you a message, the message sent out ahead of time on the screen. The statements can be as long or as short as you would like, as long as you make them work with the code that you are writing.

The Comments

As you go through and write some of your codes, you may quickly notice that it is important to add in a little reminder or a little note. This could be a kind of explanation for what you are doing in this specific part of the code. These are little notes that you would put in place because they remind you, and tell other programmers who are going through the code, what is going on at a particular part of it. It can also add some organization to the code as a whole.

The nice thing about working with these comments is that you can add them in, and with the right things in place (namely the # in front of the comment), the compiler will choose to skip right over the comment and continue with other parts of the code. This saves you time and ensures that you can add in the explanations and the notes that you want to the code without having to worry about how it will affect the code at all.

You can work through your code and write in as many of these comments as you would like. Just make sure that the comments are useful and belong there. You don't want to waste anyone's time with these comments to clutter things up and not make the whole thing look nice at all. Having too many comments is not a good thing. But if you think that your project needs it to help explain something, then go ahead and add some more in as well.

The Variables

The next thing that we are going to work on here are the variables. These are important to the Python code because you are going to find them pretty often in any code that you decide to work on. The variables are there because they can help store some of the different values that you are trying to add to the code. And when you assign a value to one of your variables, it keeps things organized and looking nice.

You can add in any value that you want to the variable, make sure that the equal sign is present so that the compiler knows where that value is meant to go. And, if you properly do the process, you can even go through and make more than one value attach to the same variable. This is done in some of the more complex codes that you may choose to work with, but it is still something that you may want to do on occasion. You need to add in the equal sign between each part to show the compiler that one variable is going to take care of more than one value at the same time.

Classes and Objects

Other topics that we can look at are the classes and the objects. Since Python is considered an object-oriented language, it is going to divide things up into classes and objects, to make it a bit easier to work with. This ensures that you can find the information that you need in the code, without a lot of hassle or worry about where it will go.

A good way to think about the classes and objects is like having a box. Each box is going to be your class, and it is responsible for holding onto certain objects. You can put as many objects inside each class as you would like, but you need to make sure that they go together in some manner. When someone takes a look in that class, it needs to make sense why they would see certain items in that class, and why certain items should be left out.

Now, the items in a class don't need to be the same, nor should you try to make them this way. But they do need to have some relation to one another and make sense for why they are in the same class as each other. Maybe you have a class of vehicles; you can put all the cars, trucks, vans, and more in there because they are all a type of vehicle for example,

This is a better way to split up the information and the data that you want to store on Python. It ensures that when you call up one of the objects that you saved, it is going to show up in the code where it is supposed to. Without this, you could run into some issues as things get lost, and it makes things more confusing for someone who is a beginner.

The Operators

The final part of the Python code that we are going to explore here is the operators. These are a great thing to learn how to work with, and even though they are simple, they are going to add a lot of power to the codes that you are doing. When you start going through your code, you will see that there are many types of operators that you can work within your code. For example, you may work with the arithmetic functions to help you any time you want to multiply, subtract, divide, and add your parts together. There are also the assignment operators that give value over to the variable, the comparison operators that will look at your different codes and determine if they go together or are similar or not and more.

Learning these operators can make writing any code that you have a lot easier. They will do comparisons, math, and assign the values that you need. And often, they use basic symbols to help get the work done. As you look through some of the codes that are going to be present throughout this guidebook, and even some of the other topics that we will talk about, you will notice a lot of these operators tend to show up, and if they weren't present, it could cause some issues with how well the code would work.

These are some of the basic parts that come with a code you would need to write in the Python language. You will need to learn how each of these works to write some of the basic codes that come with this language and make sure that you can use this language to write your codes. Even when you are working on the codes that are hard and complex to do, you may find some of these basic parts are inside as well!

Chapter 3: Working with Conditional Statements

Now, it is time to move on to the topic of conditional statements, which can also go by the name of decision control statements. These are going to be the statements that allow the computer to make some decisions, based on the input that the user has, as well as what you would like to happen with the program. You will have many times in your program where you will want the computer to make some decisions and complete itself when you are not there. If you are working on a code where you would like the user to put in their answer, rather than giving them two options to work with, then these decision control statements are going to be good options to work with.

There are going to be a few different options that you can work with when you are making these conditional statements. The three most common ones are going to include the if statement, the if else statement, and the elif statement. As a beginner, we are going to start with the basics of the if statement to get a good idea of how these can work, and then we will build up to understand some of the more complicated things that you can do with these conditional statements.

The first option that we are going to take a look at is the if statement. The if statement is going to work with the ideas and the answer that your user gives to the computer is going to be either true or false. If the user does an input of information that is seen as true based on your code, then the interpreter can continue with the program, and it will show up the statements or the information that you would like. But, if the user is on the program and puts in something that doesn't match up with your code, and is seen as false, then the program is automatically going to end.

The good news is that we can go through a bit later, and look at the steps that you can take to ensure that you are going to get the program to respond no matter what answer your user gives, but that is not what the if statement is going to focus on. We need to take a look at this simplified form for now, and then build up from there. To help us look at how the if statement is meant to look when your user interacts with it, you will need to work with the following code:

```
age = int(input("Enter your age:"))
if (age <=18):
        print("You are not eligible for voting, try next
election!")
print("Program ends")
```

Once you have added this conditional statement to your compiler, we need to explore what is going to happen with the above code. If the user does come to this part of the program, and they say that they are under the age of 18, then there will be a message that comes up on the screen. In this case, we wrote in that the message that will come up is going to be, "You are not eligible for voting, try next election!" Then the program, because we don't have any other parts of the code here right now, is going to end. But, this brings up the question of what is going to happen with this particular code if the user does say that they are older than 18?

When a computer programmer is working with the if statement, if the user puts their age in at over 18, then nothing is going to happen. The if statement is going to be the option that you use when you only want the user to pick out the one answer that your code says is true. The user has to say that they are younger than 18 in this situation, or the program is going to be done.

As you can imagine here, this is going to cause us some problems. You most likely would want to allow your user to put in any age that works for them. Some of the users who will come to this program are going to be older than 18, and you don't want the program to end without anything there because they are older than that age range. This is going to end the program before you want it to, and it doesn't look that professional with the program that you are working with when the code ends. This is a big reason why you are not going to see the if statements all that often.

But this is where we are going to bring in the if else statements and use those to fix this problem. These take the idea that we were going through, the issues that we brought up, and helping us to deal with them. Let's say that you are working with the code that we had before, and you want to make sure that your program brings up a result, no matter what answer the user decides to put into the program. You can write out an if else statement so that you can get an answer for those who are under the age of 18, and then a different answer for those who are 18 and older. The code for this expands out the option that we talked about before, but here is an example that you can use.

```
age = int(input("Enter your age:"))
if (age <=18):
        print("You are not eligible for voting, try next
election!")
else
        print("Congratulations! You are eligible to vote.
Check out your local polling station to find out more
information!)
print("Program ends")
```

This code is going to be a lot more useful to your endeavors and what you want to happen in your code, and it provides you with some more options than before. And the best part is that your code is not going to end because the user puts in their age. It is going to provide them with a statement on the screen based on the age that they put into it.

This code can also be expanded out to include some more possibilities if you would like. The example above just had two options, those under the age of 18 and those above. But you can have more options if it works for your program. For example, you can split up the age ranges a bit more if you would like. Maybe you want to know who is under the age of 18, who is in their 20's, who is in their 30's, and those who are older than 40. You can use this same idea and add in some more lines to it, to help meet the needs of your program using the if else statement.

Another example that you may want to use when it comes to the if else statement is when you ask the program to pick out their favorite color. You probably do not want to go through and write out enough code to handle each color that is out there in the world, but you will leave this open so that the user can put in the information that corresponds with their favorite color.

For this code, you may choose to have a list of six colors that you write out in the code (you can have more or less for what you need), and then you will have a message that corresponds to these six colors. You may pick out the colors of yellow, orange, green, blue, purple, and red. Then, you can add in an else statement so that the user can pick out a different color. If the user decides to have white as their favorite color here, then the seventh, and the final message will come up. This final message is going to be the same for any of the colors that don't fit in with the original six.

Adding this else statement, or the `catch all`, to the end of the code can be an important thing that you need to consider. You can't possibly list out all of the different colors that your user may choose to work with. You may take the time to put in a hundred different colors (but this takes a lot of time and code, and you won't want to do this), but then the user could go with the one color that you forget. If you don't add this else statement to the end, then the program is going to be lost at how you would like it to behave here.

The else statement is nice because it is going to be the one that you can use to catch more than one result from the user, and it can catch all of the answers that you don't account for, but that the user may choose to use. If you don't add statement in the code, then your program isn't going to be sure how to behave when the user puts that answer in.

The elif Statements

The other two options of conditional statements are going to be important for a lot of the codes that you would like to work with. The if statement is a good one to learn as a beginner getting into these statements, and they will help you to mostly get a good idea of how the conditional statements are supposed to work. These if statements are going to have a basis on the idea of the answer being either true or false.

In this case, if the answer received from the user is seen as true based on the conditions that you add to the code, then the program will see this and continue on its path. But if the condition is seen to be false, then the program is not going to have anything set up, and it is going to end. This is a simple idea to work with and is a good way to learn more about the conditional statements, but for many of the codes that you want to write out in Python, it is not going to give you the results that you want.

Then we took a look at the if else statements. These took this idea a bit further, and it understood that the ideas that come with the original if statements are going to be too simple.

These `if` `else` statements can help us handle any answer that the user will give to the system, and ensure that the program doesn't just stop. We even took a look at an example code that shows us how these kinds of statements work.

From here, we need to spend some time working on the elif statements. This is going to handle things a bit different than what the other two did, but it is still going to be useful and can add an element of fun and something different to your code. The elif statement is going to give the user a chance to pick from a few options that you present to them. And then, the answer that the user chooses is going to provide them with a predetermined statement that you added into the code.

There are different places where you can see these conditional statements. The elif statement is a unique code for the Python language, and it is often going to be used for many games, or for a different program that you would like to have with menu style of choices for the user. These statements are going to be used most often if the computer programmer would like to provide their user with some options rather than just one or two.

When you are working with these elif statements, there is a lot of freedom in what you can do with these codes. You can add in as many statements and options as you want as long as you follow the proper coding with it. Also, you should be a bit careful with adding in too many of the options. You can technically add in as many as you would like, but sometimes, it may be too much, and you may make the code unnecessarily complicated if you are adding them in without any reason. But if it works and makes sense for your code, then you can go ahead and add in as many of these as you would like.

Now that we have spent some time talking about these elif statements and what all comes with them, it is time to look at the syntax of this conditional statement to get a better idea of how it works, and when you are most likely to use it. A good example of the syntax with the conditional elif statement will include:

```
if expression1:
statement(s)
elif expression2:
statement(s)
elif expression3:
statement(s)
else:
statement(s)
```

This is a pretty basic syntax of the elif statement, and you can add in as many of these statements as you would like. Just take that syntax and then place the right information into each part and the answer that is listed next to it. Notice that there is also an else statement at the end of this. Don't forget to add this to your code so that it can catch any answer that the user puts in that isn't listed in your elif statements.

To help you better understand how these elif statements work, and how the syntax above is going to work, let's take a look at a little game that you can create using these statements:

```
Print("Let's enjoy a Pizza! Ok, let's go inside Pizzahut!")
print("Waiter, Please select Pizza of your choice from the menu")
pizzachoice = int(input("Please enter your choice of Pizza:"))
if pizzachoice == 1:
     print('I want to enjoy a pizza napoletana')
elif pizzachoice == 2:
     print('I want to enjoy a pizza rustica')
elif pizzachoice == 3:
     print('I want to enjoy a pizza capricciosa')
else:
     print("Sorry, I do not want any of the listed pizza's, please bring a Coca Cola for me.")
```

With this example, the user will be able to look at the choices, and then choose what they would like to get from the menu. If you set this up, the corresponding statement is going to come up with the option that they use. For example, if the user would like to order a *pizza rustica*, they would click on the number 2. If they would instead go with a drink, then they can do that as well. While we were working with some examples of pizza here, you can easily use this syntax and the ideas behind it to make the menu the way that you would like and provide your user with some options as well.

There are a lot of different things that you can do when it comes to using conditional statements in your code. They provide a lot of options and a ton more power while still being easy enough for a beginner to get started with. These conditional statements are going to make it easier for you to get the program to make a decision based on the input given from the user, without the programmer having to figure out all of the possible scenarios or having to be there ahead of time.

There are a lot of times when you can use conditional statements and some of the syntaxes that we have discussed in this guidebook. Open up your compiler and practice a few of them to help you get started on the right foot with using these for your own needs and programs as well.

Chapter 4: How Do Loops Work?

Another important topic to explore when we are working with the Python coding language is the idea of the loop. These are important to a lot of the codes that you will need to write, and sometimes, they can help with those conditional statements as well. One of the best things about these loops is that they can get a lot of information into a few lines, which helps to clean up your code and makes it powerful without having to write out a lot of information.

Often, you will start to bring up these loops any time when you are writing out a code where you would like to have a particular program repeat something. Even if it is a few times, this can work as well, but you don't want to mess up the code or waste your time writing that part out a few times. While it may not seem like a big deal to write out that part of the code two or three times to get it to repeat, there could potentially be times when you want to write out the code a hundred times or more. Instead of writing out a hundred lines, or multiple lines a hundred times, you would be able to utilize these loops and get it done in just a few lines. A loop is what you need to handle this work, and you will like how easy and clean it looks.

For example, you may be working on a code, and then you get to a point where you would like to have the numbers listed out from one to ten for you. Of course, this can take up a lot of code and space if you tried to write this out each time you wanted a number listed. But with a loop, you would be able to set it to continue counting up until it reached the conditions that you set ahead of time.

This sounds like it is hard, and as a beginner, you may be worried about how you would be able to do it for yourself. These loops are going to tell your compiler that it needs to repeat the same line or lines of code over and over again until the inserted conditions are met. If you would like to get the code to count from one to ten, then you would tell the compiler that the condition is when the output is higher than ten. Don't worry about this being too confusing; we are going to show you a few examples of how this can work in a moment.

Of course, when you are writing out the loop codes, you must make sure that you put in some condition that will end the loop. Beginners can often forget to set up this condition to end the program, and then they end up in some trouble. The code will keep going through the loop, getting stuck because it doesn't know when it is supposed to stop. You must make sure that you add in a break or a condition to the code so that it knows when it should stop and move on to some of the other things that should be done in the code.

With some of the other methods of traditional coding that we have talked about, or that you may have used in the past, you would have to avoid these loops and write out each line of the code. Even if there were some parts of the code that were similar, or you were retrying the same piece of code to make a pattern show up, this is how a beginner would have to do the work to get it done. This is a tedious process that takes a lot of time, and it is hard to do.

The good news is that you can get these loops and put them to work, ensuring that you can combine a few lines of code and get the compiler to read through it again until conditions are met, rather than having you rewrite the code that many times. This means that instead of writing out potentially hundreds of lines of code, you can write out a few and have the compiler read through it again until it is done.

These loops are so important and helpful when it comes to working with the Python language, and it is well worth your time, even as a beginner, to learn how to use it properly. With that in mind, there are several types of loops that you can work with to help you make your code easier to write and save a lot of space and time when writing the code.

Each of these loops is going to be helpful and can be used in different circumstances based on what you are trying to get done in the code. The three main types of loops that we are going to explore through the rest of this guidebook include the while loop, the for loop, and the nested loop.

Working with Our while Loop

So, out of the three loops that we can work with, we will start with the while loop in the Python language. The while loop is a good choice to make if you have a predetermined number of times you would like the code to cycle through that line. You can set this up ahead of time, and ensure that the loop goes through it that many times, no more and no less.

When you use the while loop, the goal here is not to allow the code to go through the cycle as many times as it wants, or an indefinite number of times, but you do want to make sure that it goes through five, or six, or however, many times are needed. If you want the program to count from one to ten, for example, then you would set up the loop to do its work ten times. It also makes sure that the loop happens one time, and then checks the conditions before doing it again. With this option, the loop will put the number one on the screen, check the conditions, and then do number two through to ten.

This is a lot to take in and may be hard to understand. The sample code below is a good way to see what the while loop is all about and check what is going to happen when you try to write it out in your compiler

```
counter = 1
while(counter <= 3):
        principal   =   int(input("Enter   the   principal
amount:"))
        numberofyeras = int(input("Enter   the   number   of
years:"))
        rateofinterest = float(input("Enter   the   rate   of
interest:"))
        simpleinterest  =  principal  *  numberofyears  *
rateofinterest/100
        print("Simple interest = %.2f" %simpleinterest)
        #increase the counter by 1
        counter = counter + 1
        print("You  have  calculated  simple  interest  for  3
time!")
```

Before we move on, take this code and add it to your compiler and let it execute this code. You will see that when this is done, the output is going to come out in a way that the user can place any information that they want into the program. Then the program will do its computations and figure out the interest rates, as well as the final amounts based on whatever numbers the user placed into the system.

With the completed example, we can set up a loop that would go through its iterations three times. This means that the user can get the results they want before the system decides to move on. As the computer programmer, you can go through this and add in more iterations, and have the loop repeat itself more if you want it to based on what is the best option for your program.

Understanding the for Loop

There are a lot of times when you may work with the while loop that we discussed above. It is going to be a great option any time that you would like to work with a loop, and often it is the only choice that you need. But, there will be some times when this loop is not going to be quite right, and you will need to change it up a little bit. The for loop is the option that you should choose here. This is considered the traditional method for loops so that you can use it in many different situations.

When you bring out the for loop, you have to make sure that it is set up in a way that the user isn't the one that has to provide the program with information on when to stop the loop. Instead, this loop is going to be set up in a way that it goes over the iteration in the order that things show up in the statement. And then, as it reads through the statement, this information is going to show up on the screen. This can nicely work because it isn't going to need any outside force or any outside user to input information in. A good example of how this code is going to loop when you write it out includes:

```
# Measure some strings:
words = ['apple,' 'mango,' 'banana,' 'orange']
for w in words:
print(w, len(w))
```

When you work with the for above loop example, you can add it to your compiler and see what happens when it gets executed. When you do this, the four fruits that come out on your screen will show up in the exact order that you have them written out. If you would like to have them show up in a different order, you can do that, but then you need to go back to your code and rewrite them in the right order, or your chosen order. Once you have then written out in the syntax and they are ready to be executed in the code, you can't make any changes to them.

The Nested Loop

And the third type of loop that can work well when you write codes in the Python language is known as the nested loop. You will find that this one is going to work a bit different than the for, and the while loops that we did, but it can be useful in many different situations. When you decide to write out a nested loop in your code, you are taking a loop, whether it is a for or a while loop, and then placing it inside of another one. Then, the original loop and the second loop will continue to run until both are done.

This may seem like a lot of work to add in another loop to your code, but there are times when you will work on a code, and this is needed. For example, maybe you have a code that is going to include a multiplication table. It would be a lot of work and wasted time to type out all of the numbers and everything that you need for the multiplication table, getting it to go from 1*1 up to ten times ten.

That is a lot of code to think about, and whether you are a beginner or a professional with coding languages, you won't want to go through and do all of this. The good news is that the nested loop is going to handle this for you. With the help of a nested loop, you can get all of the numbers in this multiplication chart or table to show up, and it is all going to be done in a few lines of code. The way that this is going to look will include the following:

```
#write a multiplication table from 1 to 10
For x in xrange(1, 11):
        For y in xrange(1, 11):
        Print '%d = %d' % (x, y, x*x)
```

When you got the output of this program, it is going to look similar to this:

```
1*1  =  1
1*2  =  2
1*3  =  3
1*4  =  4
```

Up to `1*10  =  2`

Then, it would move on to do the table by twos such as this:

```
2*1  =2
2*2  =  4
```

And so on until you end up with `10*10  =  100` as your final spot in the sequence.

Go ahead and put this into the compiler and see what happens. You will have four lines of code, and end up with a whole multiplication table that shows up on your program. Think of how many lines of code you would have to write out to get this table the traditional way that you did before? This table only took a few lines to accomplish, which shows how powerful and great the nested loop can be.

As you can see from the above information, these loops are going to be fantastic options that you can add into your code.

There are many reasons that you would need to add a loop into the code that you are writing, but you can quickly see how it can add a lot of information into a few lines of code, making your work faster and saving you a lot of hassle and potential mistakes along the way. Practice each of these loops a little bit so that you gain some more familiarity with how each of them works, and help you to learn when you are the most likely to use them in your code.

Chapter 5: Writing an Exception in Your Code

The next thing is how you can handle, and even raise, some of your exceptions in the code. As you work through writing some of your codes, you will find that the Python program already has a few of its exceptions that it can bring out if you or the user does something it doesn't approve of. And on top of that, there are some that the computer programmer can add into the code, to ensure that the code is going to work the way that you would like.

If the exception is considered an automatic one, then you can find it inside of your Python library. An excellent example of this one is when the user decides to divide by zero. This is something that the Python code doesn't like, and it won't allow it to happen. If the user does try to do this, then the exception from the Python library is going to show up here. If you are raising one of your exceptions, then you need to go through and tell the computer to act in that manner.

While these are important depending on the code that we want to work with, the first type that we are going to explore are the ones that the compiler will automatically recognize without you doing anything in the code. If the user does do something that will raise the exception, then the program won't let them go through. This could happen if you add in a statement that isn't right for the code, or you misspell a class so that the compiler is not able to pull it up. Or, again, it could be when you or the user are going on the program, and you try to divide something by zero. These are a few examples of the exception that the compiler is going to recognize, and will try to raise for you automatically.

As the computer programmer in Python, it is a good idea to know about the different exceptions that are going to appear in the library of Python for you. This helps because it will tell you what you need to change up in the code, and can give you a heads up about when one of these exceptions are going to turn up in the code. Some of the exceptions that the compiler may bring up for you along with their keywords include:

Finally—this is the action that you will want to use to perform cleanup actions, whether the exceptions occur or not.

Assert—this condition is going to trigger the exception inside of the code

Raise—the raise command is going to trigger an exception manually inside of the code.

Try/except—this is when you want to try out a block of code, and then it is recovered. Thanks to the exceptions that either you or the Python code raised.

Can I Raise My Exceptions in the Code?

Yes, it is perfectly acceptable to go through and raise some of your exceptions based on what you are trying to write for your program. But first, we shall look at how you can use these exceptions in any code that you try to write. When the automatic ones, the ones that the compiler is going to understand come up, you want to make sure that you are prepared, and what you can do to make sure that it is easier to understand for the user.

If you are going through on your code, and you notice that some issue shows up, or you would like to figure out why this program is doing something that seems wrong, then you may take a look at the compiler and see that it is trying to raise a new exception for you. This is because the program has had a chance to take a look at the code and is trying to figure out how you would like to fix something that shouldn't be happening.

The good news is that a lot of the issues that are going to show up with this are going to be simple and easy to fix. For example, you may try to bring out a file that you created, but you misspelled it or gave it the wrong name, either when you first named it or when you are trying to bring it back up. Since the compiler cannot find the name, it is going to raise an exception for this.

A good way to get a look at how this exception is going to work; we are going to stop here and look at an example of what it looks like when the compiler raises one of these exceptions. Add the following code into your compiler so that you can get an idea of what happens when an exception shows up in your code:

```
x = 10
y = 10
result = x/y #trying to divide by zero
print(result)
```

The output that you are going to get when you try to get the interpreter to go through this code would be:

```
>>>
Traceback (most recent call last):
        File "D: \Python34\tt.py", line 3, in <module>
        result = x/y
ZeroDivisionError: division by zero
>>>
```

When you stop and look at this example and ask it to execute, the compiler is then going to bring up a nice error message on the screen. This is because the user tried to divide things by zero. Most coding languages, including Python, are not going to allow this to happen, and so the error is going to be raised.

Now, you could leave this how it is in the code, without making changes. But when you go through and leave it this way, and the user tries to divide by zero, they are going to get a quite long and messy error message. This is going to be hard to understand and often comes with a series of letters and numbers that they are not going to understand. As the programmer, you can go through with this and make some changes so that the code explains what is wrong, and the user can then make some changes. Rather than leaving them confused when a long and messy error message shows up when they do something wrong, you can use a code like the following to help show what the user did exactly to upset the compiler at this point:

```
x = 10
y = 0
result = 0
try:
       result = x/y
       print(result)
except ZeroDivisionError:
       print("You are trying to divide by zero.")
```

With this example, the code we are adding to the compiler is going to be similar to the first example that we tried to do. But with this one, there are a few changes so that the message explains what is going on any time that the user does raise the exception that is to blame here. You can add in any message that you would like at this point, but this message has to do except trying to divide by zero.

How Do I Define My Exceptions Inside a Code?

Now, as earlier discussed, the previous examples were to show us how we can manage an exception that showed up naturally in the code itself. These are ones that the Python code is not going to allow because they don't conform to things that the code can do. We also looked at some of the steps that you can take to change up the message and personalize it to the error at hand, rather than trying to have a string of letters and numbers that don't make a lot of sense.

But we can take a step further. You can raise some exceptions in the code that are all your own. These are things that the code would normally see as just fine, but which won't work based on the program that you are creating, and some of the things that you would like the code to do. You can easily raise these exceptions in the code as well if you would like.

For example, maybe you are working on a code or a kind of game, and you decide you want to allow the user to input a few types of numbers or a certain number of chances, and that is it. This can work well with some of the games or the applications that you want to create. If the user takes up all of their turns or they are not picking the right numbers to place into space, then there needs to be an error message or an exception that is going to show up in the process.

These exceptions can be fun because they are unique to the code that you are writing. You need to take some time to write them into the code that you are working on though because, since they are your exceptions, the compiler is not going to recognize them without this, and will continue to read through the rest of the code. One way that you can write out this exception in your code would include the following:

```
class CustomException(Exception):
def_init_(self, value):
    self.parameter = value
def_str_(self):
    return repr(self.parameter)


try:
    raise CustomException("This is a CustomError!")
except CustomException as ex:
    print("Caught:", ex.parameter)
```

When you finish this particular code, you are done successfully adding in your exception. When someone does raise this exception, the message "Caught: This is a CustomError!" will come up on the screen. You can always change the message to show whatever you would like, but this was there as a placeholder to show what we are doing. Take a moment here to add this to the compiler and see what happens.

And it is as easy as that. You can go through and create any exception that you would like in your code, as long as you use the formula that is above to help you do it. You can go through and make some changes to the wording and the statements that you would like to see show up on the exceptions that you have. This can help make it more unique for your ongoing project.

Exception handling is a good topic to learn more about, and as you work to write out the more advanced codes, rather than some of the basic beginner codes that are available. There are a lot of times where you will want to either create your exceptions to the code to make your program work the way that you would like or learn how to handle some of the exceptions that the computer recognizes on its own.

Working with some of the codes that we discussed in this chapter, and spending some time adding them to the compiler and seeing what happens when you change up little things in the code can make a big difference in how quickly you can get started with this and see the results that you would like. Make sure that you practice a bit so that you are ready to work with any of the exceptions that you would like in Python, and to learn exactly how these exceptions are meant to work.

Chapter 6: Working with User-Defined Functions When You Work with Python

Functions are going to be something that many different coding languages are going to share in common. It is going to be a block of code that you can recycle to help you to work on a specific task. However, when you take some time to define one of these functions in python, you have to understand what the two main types of functions are, or you are going to run into some troubles along the way—and these two types are going to include the built-in functions and the user-defined functions.

The first kind, or the built-in functions, are going to be the ones that come with Python, the ones that are found in the libraries of this coding language. But you can define some of your functions, based on your project, and these are the user-defined functions. In Python, all of the functions will need to be treated like objects, which can often make things a lot easier to work with, as you will see in a moment.

As we go through this chapter, we will spend some time focusing on the user-defined functions and how you will be able to use these for your projects. To make this kind of concept a bit easier to work with, we are going to bring in some examples of how to work with these user-defined functions. Before we do that, though, let's look below and figure out a few of the important concepts that are needed to make more sense of these user-defined functions.

Why Are User-Defined Functions So Important?

To keep it simple, in most cases, the developer can write out a code to have their user-defined functions, or, if you are a beginner in this, you can use a third-party library that helps out with these. Sometimes, these functions are going to provide you with a distinct advantage, and some neat things that you can do, depending on the way you would like to use them up in the code. However, there are going to be some things that a developer will have to remember about these functions and the way they work in your code, including:

These functions are going to be made out of reusable code blocks. It is necessary only to write them out once, and then you can use them as many times as you need in the code. You can even take that user-defined function and use it in some of your other applications as well.

These functions can also be very useful. You can use them to help with anything you want from writing out specific logic in business to working on common utilities. You can also modify them based on your requirements to make the program work properly.

The code is often going to be friendly for developers, easy to maintain, and well-organized all at once. This means that you can support the approach for modular design.

You can write out these types of functions independently. And the tasks of your project can be distributed for rapid application development if needed.

A user-defined function that is thoughtfully and well-defined can help ease the process for the development of an application.

Now that we know a little bit more about the basics of a user-defined function, it is time to look at some of the different arguments that can come with these functions before moving on to some of the codes that you can use with this function.

Now that we have looked over these user-defined functions, it is time to take a look at the arguments of the functions that you can use. This ensures that you can get your code to do the things that you want. We will even look at some of the different codes that are available with these user-defined functions so that you end up with the results that you would like.

The Arguments of Functions Available

Any time that a computer programmer is working on a particular code in Python, these user-defined functions will be able to take on the argument of four different types. These argument types, as well as their corresponding meanings, are already defined ahead of time, and it is not something that the developer can change on their own. Instead, the developer will need to go through and follow these rules. And when they are ready, the developer can also add in a few things or take away a few things to create the customized functions that they want. There are going to be four arguments that you can use with your functions, and these will include:

The default argument: The Python coding language is going to have its way of representing the values of the default and the syntax that you are using for these kinds of arguments. These values are going to help indicate that the argument is going to take a particular value—unless you pass on a different value during the call. You will be able to tell what the default value is with the help of the equal sign.

Required arguments: These types of arguments are the ones that have to be present, the ones that are seen as mandatory for the function to work. You need to make sure that the values you are using are passed in the right order, and in the right numbers, any time that function is called out. If this doesn't happen, then the code won't work for you.

The keyword arguments: The third option of arguments that you can work with here are known as the keyword arguments. These are going to be relevant to the function calls, and they are the keywords that are going to be mentioned here, along with the values that have been assigned to them. These are the keywords that are mapped with the function arguments, which will make it easier on the programmer to identify what the right value is, even if there is a reason why the order doesn't stay where it is supposed to be. This is a good argument to use because it ensures that everything is going to stay organized in the code.

A variable number of arguments: This is another argument that you can use if you are working on a function, but you don't know exactly how many arguments need to be passed on to the function. Or you can take this one and design it in a way where the number of arguments can be passed as long as the requirements you set are met.

Writing Out Your User-Defined Functions

Now that we have spent a bit of time looking at these user-defined functions and what they are all about, it is time to learn some of the codes that need to happen inside Python to create one of your own. There are going to be four basic steps that you can follow to ensure that a user-defined function is going to appear when you are done.

Remember with this one; you have the power to make it as simple or as difficult as you would like. Of course, in this guidebook, and this chapter, we are going to look at the basics of what would need to occur to ensure your user-defined function is created. The steps that you will need to follow to make this happen includes:

Go through and declare the function. You can declare your function with the help of the "def" keyword, and then you need to have the name of the function shown up after announcing the keyword.

Now, you can write out the arguments: These arguments need to be inside the two parentheses of the function. You can then end the whole declaration with a colon so that you are following the right protocol that comes with Python.

Add in the statements that you would like the program to execute for you at this time.

And finally, you can end the function. You can decide whether you would like to go with a return statement or not with this one.

Now that we know a bit more about the steps that you can take to get your function written and ready to go with this, it is time to make one of your user-defined functions. A good example of how you would do this includes:

```
def userDefFunction (arg1, arg2, arg3, …):
     program statement1
     program statement2
     program statement3
     ...
     Return;
```

And that is all! Follow these steps, and you can create any user-defined functions that you would like to add some power, and some uniqueness to the program that you are writing.

Chapter 7: Inheritances in the Python Code

In this chapter, we shall consider another fantastic thing that you can do in the Python coding language. This technique is called an inheritance. When you take a look at some of the codes and examples that we will provide in this chapter, it may seem a bit overwhelming at first. Some of the codes are a bit longer and look like they are complicated. The good news is that these inheritances are much easier to use than you might think, and they can take a lot of big and bulky code and make it easier to write, without having to type out a ton of lines in the process. This can ensure that the coding looks nicer, can clean up the work that you do, and still provides you with all of the results that you are looking for in your program.

So, let's get started by writing our inheritances. To help you out here, and make sure that the inheritance is going to stay as simple as possible, we first need to come up with the definition of what inheritance is all about. This inheritance is going to be when you take all or part of your original code, which is going to be called the parent code in this technique, and then copy it down and make some changes to come up with a child code.

There are a lot of things that you can do with these child codes. You can adjust them, add to them, and take away from them as you wish. This changes and adds things to this part of the code but will not affect the parent code as long as you properly did the inheritance. And you can make as many of these child inheritances, based on the original parent class, as you would like, changing and adding to each part as you would like.

As a beginner, this may sound like it is pretty complex, and is going to be hard for you to work with. But we will walk through a few examples of the codes that you can do with it, and you will find that it can be incredibly useful. You can copy down the parent code as much as you want, and then add and take away what is needed to ensure the code works how you want. To understand how this is going to work in your code, let's take a look at the following syntax and example of inheritance.

```
#Example of inheritance
#base class
class Student(object):
        def__init__(self, name, rollno):
        self.name = name
        self.rollno = rollno
#Graduate class inherits or derived from Student class
class GraduateStudent(Student):
        def__init__(self, name, rollno, graduate):
        Student__init__(self, name, rollno)
        self.graduate = graduate
```

```
def DisplayGraduateStudent(self):
    print"Student Name:", self.name)
    print("Student Rollno:", self.rollno)
    print("Study Group:", self.graduate)

#Post Graduate class inherits from Student class
class PostGraduate(Student):
    def__init__(self, name, rollno, postgrad):
    Student__init__(self, name, rollno)
    self.postgrad = postgrad

    def DisplayPostGraduateStudent(self):
    print("Student Name:", self.name)
    print("Student Rollno:", self.rollno)
    print("Study Group:", self.postgrad)

#instantiate from Graduate and PostGraduate classes
    objGradStudent = GraduateStudent("Mainu", 1, "MS-
Mathematics")
    objPostGradStudent  =  PostGraduate("Shainu",  2,
"MS-CS")
    objPostGradStudent.DisplayPostGraduateStudent()
```

When you type this into your interpreter, you are going to get the results:

```
('Student Name:,' 'Mainu')
('Student Rollno:,' 1)
('Student Group:,' 'MSC-Mathematics')
```

```
('Student Name:,' 'Shainu')
('Student Rollno:,' 2)
('Student Group:,' 'MSC-CS')
```

The inheritance is a nice technique to learn how to work with because it adds in a lot of freedom when trying to write out a new code. If you have either a parent class or a base class that has a lot of the features that you would like to work with, or that you want to use to make the derived or the child class, then the inheritance is the way to work on this without having to rewrite the code all of those times. If you have one child class, this may not seem like that big of a deal. But if you have to do this ten, twenty, or more times in your code, it is going to save a lot of time and ensure that your program still looks nice.

It is possible that the programmer can go through and start with one parent class and create as many of the child classes as they would like. As long as they are done with one another, and you work with a syntax similar to what we have above, it is possible to add in as many of these child classes as are needed for your project.

This can make the code look nicer, can make the writing of the code easier, limit the amount that you are going to need to write out, and it ensures that you can get a new program written as quickly as possible. Each of these new derived classes can take on any of the features that it wants from that parent class, or it can even drop some of the parts if it wishes. This helps you to continue on the code, and make it work the way you would like.

Can I Override My Base Class?

Now that we have had talked about how the inheritance works with your code and some of the benefits of using inheritance, it is time to move on to the next step, which is learning how to override one of the base classes and make it work for this process.

There are going to be times when you will work with a specific derived class, and then you find that it is time to override the things that are found inside of it when you make the inheritance. When this happens, you need to do a few steps to override the actions that are found in that base class. This means that the computer programmer needs to look through their base class and change up the behavior that is found inside. This makes it easier for the derived class to get the behavior that you want and nothing else.

Don't let the idea of overriding the base class seem complicated. It is a nice way to look at the features that are in the parental class and decide which ones are going to go on to the new child class, and which ones you are going to keep behind. This also ensures that you can keep the parent class in the same place without those changes affecting it and the way your code is going to behave.

Overloading

One of the other things that a computer programmer can do when they want to work with these inheritances is a process that is called overloading. When you are working with this process, you are taking an identifier and using it to help define more than one method at the same time. Many times, this is going to be up to two methods inside each class, but you may run across a situation where it needs to define three or more in the process.

The two methods to use for this same identifier need to be inside the same class, and then the parameters need to be different for this to work. You will find that the process of overloading is going to work the best when you want to have them do a task that needs to fit with different parameters.

Overloading is not one of those processes that a beginner is going to have much use for as a beginner. But, as you work on more programs and more codes along the way, you may find more uses for it. Learning a bit about overloading and what it means can make things easier when you get started with the idea of inheritances.

A Final Note About Inheritances

As you decide to work on some inheritances inside this coding language, it is possible you will find that you can move on to multiple inheritances at the same time. When it is time to work with multiple inheritance components, you will find that as you go through each of the levels, they are all going to have similarities to one another, but you are still going through each one and making the small additions or changes that you need for each level.

With these multiple inheritances, you will notice that they are going to be pretty similar to that single inheritance that we were talking about before. But instead of stopping at just one, you will continue down through the line, adding in more things or taking away more things as you progress through the code. You will turn the derived class over to the parent class and continue through this process.

When you are working on a code, and you notice that it wants you to work with multiple inheritances to get the work done, you will need to start with one class, which is your base class, and then it will have at least two parent classes to help you out.

This is important to learn because it makes things easier when you need to borrow a few features from more than one part of the code that you have.

Multiple inheritances can be as simple or as complicated as you would like to make them. When you work on them, you can create a brand new class, which we will call Class C, and you got the information to create this new class from the previous one, or Class B. You can go back and find that Class B was the one that you created from information out of Class A. Each of these layers is going to contain some features that you like from the class ahead of it, and you can go as far as possible into it as you would like. Depending on the code that you decide to write, you could have ten or more of these classes, each level having features from the previous one to keep it going.

While creating these inheritance components, remember that you are not allowed to move from multiple inheritance components over to a circular inheritance. You can add in as many of your parent classes as needed to the code, but you can't make it go in a circle and connect things with this method.

As you start to write out some more codes inside the Python language, you will find that working with different types of inheritances can be pretty popular. There are many times when you can stick with the same block of code in the program, and then make some changes without having to waste your time rewriting the code over and over again.

Chapter 8: Working with the Python Generators

The next topic that we are going to explore a bit is going to be the Python generators. They are a type of function that is meant to help you create a sequence of results. These generators are great because they can maintain their local state, allowing the function to resume where it left off any time that it is called up more than once. You should think of this generator in a way similar to the iterator. The function state can be maintained with a simple keyword of "Yield." In Python, you can think of this as typing in "return," but we are going to explore some of the differences that come up with this.

How Does a Generator Work?

There are a lot of different things that these generators can do to help make your code as strong as possible. But the best way for a beginner to learn more about generators and how they are meant to work will be to look at an example like the one below:

```
# generator_example_1.py

Def numberGenerator(n):
    Number = 0
```

```
    While number < n:
    Yield number
    Number + = 1

myGenerator = numberGenerator(3)

print(next(myGenerator))
print(next(myGeneartor))
print(next(myGenerator))
```

The above code is going to be put into the compiler and defines the generator for you. In specific, it is going to define the generator that goes under the name of "numberGenerator," and it is going to provide you with a value of 'n' as the argument. This happens before you can go through all of this, and define it with the help of a while loop to help with limiting the value. Also, this is all going to go through and help when it is time to define a variable that comes with the name of "number," and it can then assign the zero value back to this.

Any time you want to use the 'myGenerator' to bring up an instantiated generator with the next() method, it is going to go through and run the generator through the whole code until you get to the 'yield' statement. For example, this is going to return 1 to you. Even when you do get the value returned in this scenario, your function is going to try and keep the variable written as 'number" when you call up the function next, but it will let the value grow by one. What this means is that this is going to start up again right where it left off, and the next time the function is going to be called up, it will continue from there.

If you were doing this and you wanted to call up your generator more than once following that code written above, then you will find that it raises an exception (remember we talked about those exceptions a bit earlier on). It is going to say "StopIteration" since the generator is done, and it has finished up and reverted out from that internal while loop it was doing.

This is a strong thing to see in the code sometimes, but the functionality is very useful because you will be able to work with these generators to help you create any of the iterable components that you would like.

The Differences in "Between" and "Yield"

Now, there are a few times when you will want to change up the keyword that you are using. Sometimes, you will need to use the return keyword. This is used when you would like to get a return of a value from the given function. And when you do use it, the function is going to get lost out of the local state.

This means that once you go back and try to call up that function for the second time, then the function got lost, and it is going to restart from the first statement.

If that is what you would like the function to do, then this is not a bit problem. But, you can also work with the yield keyword to help keep the state between the different calls of the functions. This method is helpful because it ensures that after you are doing using it, the function is going to go back from where it was first called up. This is a good one to choose depending on the place you want your function to end up when all is said and done.

How Do I Use the return in a Generator?

The generator can use the statement for 'return' but only when there isn't a `return`value. The generator will then go on as in any other function return when it reaches this statement. The return tells the program that you are done and you want it to go back to the rest of the code. Let's take a look at how you can change up the code to use these generators by adding in an if else clause so that you can discriminate against any numbers that are above 20. The code you would use for this includes:

```
# geneator_example_2.py
```

```
def numberGeneator(n):
    if n < 20:
    number = 0
    while number < n:
    yield number
    number +=1
else:
    return
print(list(numberGeneator(30)))
```

This particular example is going to show that the genitor will be an empty array. This is because we have set it so that it won't yield any values that are above 20. Since 30 is above 20, you will not get any results with this one. In this particular case, the return statement is going to work in the same way as a break statement. But, if you go through this code and you get a value that is below 20, you would then see that show up in the code.

Additional Information That You Need to Know About Generators

When you are working with these generators, you should remember that it is going to be a new type of iterator, one that the Python code has already gone through and defined with the notation of a function so that it all becomes easier to use.

When you work with these generators, you are working with a function type that is going to give you a yield expression.

Now, these are not going to get you a return value if that is what you want. However, when you use these, they are going to give you the results that you are looking for. The process to help you call out the generator is going to be considered a process that is automatic in Python. The context that you need to use is going to be the value that your local variables have, the location of the needed control flows, and other factors as well.

Now, there are some options when it comes to calling up the generator that you want to use. If you call it with the help of __next__, the yield you are going to get will show up at the next iteration value in the line. You can also choose to work with __iter__, which is one that will automatically implement in your program, and it tells the program that it should take that generator and use it in the best place where an iterator is needed.

As a programmer, there are a few options that you can choose from when it comes to working on these generators. Some of the options that you can use include:

Generator expressions: These types of expressions give you as the programmer the ability to define a generator with a simple notation. This is done when you are creating your list in Python. You would use the methods of __iter__ and __next__ because they provide you the results for any objects in the generator type.

Recursive generators: It is possible for your chosen generator to be recursive, just like what you would find with some functions. The idea here is that you would swap all of the elements that are on your list with the one on top, allowing all of them to move to the first position, and the rest of the list is then gone.

Are There Specific Times When I Should Work with a Generator?

One question that some beginners are going to have when they go through this chapter is when they should consider working with a generator in their code. As we have seen through some of the examples and the things we have talked about in this chapter, the generators can be more advanced tools that are needed to write out the code that you have. In programming with the Python language, there can be times when these generators are useful, and they can improve the efficiency of your code. Some of the scenarios about when you would need to work with these generators will include

Any time that you are working with a lot of data that needs to be processed through, generators are going to be helpful because they can calculate instantly. This is often the process used with stream processing.

You can also work with what is known as stacked generators with the pipping process. This is when you would be able to use generators to pipeline a series of operations so that things are as easy as possible in your code.

Chapter 9: What Are the Regular Expressions?

Any time you are ready to work on some codes in the Python language, one thing that you may notice about all of this is that Python comes with a great library. This Python library is going to contain a lot of the things that you need to write the code, including regular expressions, and it is going to be at least partly responsible for handling the searches you want to do while also taking care of the different coding tasks that need to happen behind the scenes.

You will be able to take and use these regular expressions in the code to help you filter out the different strings of text or individual parts of the text. It is possible to check and see if a string or some other text is already inside the code, and whether or not it is going to match up with some of the regular expressions as well. The nice thing about these regular expressions is that you can stick with a similar syntax, no matter the language you choose to go with. So, if you learn how to get this done inside the Python language, you can take the knowledge and work with regular expressions in other languages as well.

By this point, we have talked about some of the benefits of regular expressions, but we haven't explored what these expressions are all about, or even how you will be able to use these regular expressions inside your code. A good place to start for this process and help you to understand is to bring out your text editor, and then try to get the program to locate any word that was spelled in two different manners in the code. These regular expressions can be used to cut out the errors and the confusion that could come up with this problem.

You will quickly see that working with these regular expressions can open up a world of different things that you can do with the code you have on hand and are writing. This is why learning how to use these regular expressions properly is going to be so important. If you would like to bring out these expressions and start using them in your code, the first thing that you need to do is import the expression library. Do this when you first start to install Python because you are likely to use these regular expressions quite a bit.

There are a lot of different regular expressions that a computer programmer can choose from when they want to write out their statements. And if you know ahead of time how these statements work and all of the things that they can do, it is going to make a big difference on what you can make your code do. Let's spend a bit of time here looking at the regular expressions that are the most common, how these expressions work, and how you can use them properly in your code.

The Basic Patterns Present

One thing that a lot of computer programmers like about these regular expressions is that they aren't stuck with just having them present for one fixed character. These regular expressions are going to help you watch out for some of the patterns needed along the way. As you work on these regular expressions, you may notice that some of the most common patterns that show up include:

a, X, 9, < -- ordinary characters match themselves exactly. The meta-characters that aren't going to match themselves simply because they have a special meaning include: . ^ $ * ? { [ ] and more.

. (the period)—this is going to match any single except the new line symbol of '\n'

\w—this is the lowercase w that is going to match the "word" character. This can be a letter, a digit, or an underscore. Keep in mind that this is the mnemonic, and it is going to match a single word character rather than the whole word.

\b—this is the boundary between a non-word and a word.

\s—this is going to match a single white space character, including the form, tab, return, newline, and even space. If you do \S, you are talking about any character that is not a white space.

^ = start, $ = end—these are going to match to the end or the start of your string.

\t, \n, \r—these are going to stand for tab, newline, and return

\d—this is the decimal digit for all numbers between 0 and 9. Some of the older regex utilities will not support this so be careful when using it

\ --this is going to inhibit how special the character is. If you use this if you are uncertain about whether the character has some special meaning or not to ensure that it is treated like another character.

Of course, these are a sampling of the different regular expressions that you can bring out and use inside your codes. Make sure to try them out a few times because they are important, and you need to gain some experience with them to ensure they work properly in your code. There are many different instances and types of codes that will need these regular expressions, and there are even times when you will need more than one to get the results you would like in the code.

Doing Queries in Python with the Help of Regular Expressions

Now, not only are you able to use these regular expressions to help you find basic patterns in the code that you have, but it is also possible to use these as a way to search for any input string inside the code. There are going to be three methods available for you to do these searches, based on what you are trying to find in the code. Each code and each part of the code is going to require you to do a different query type to get things to work. Let's take a look at each of these three, and get a better idea of how each one does work.

The Search Method

The first query option we shall consider is the search method. This one is helpful to use because it is going to allow the programmer to match up the query, no matter where it shows up in the code to start with. This function isn't going to come with as many restrictions as the other two we will talk about. If you would like to search for a word or a few words throughout the whole string, and not just at the beginning of it or the end of the string, then the search method is the one that you will want to work with.

When you utilize this search method, it is going to help look for a word or a statement that shows up inside your string. It doesn't matter where this item shows up, even if it is the last part of the whole string. An excellent example of what this is going to look like when you type it into your compiler includes

```
import re
string = 'apple, orange, mango, orange'
match = re.search(r'orange', string)
print(match.group(0))
```

Before we move on with this one, open up your compiler and add this code in to see the output. This code is, if you did it properly, it's going to provide you with the output of "orange.' For this method, we are going to see the match show up just one time, regardless of how many times the term comes in the code. So, with this one, you technically see the word orange show up twice, but the search method is going only to bring it up once. As soon as the method can find this term the first time, it is going to stop looking and will provide you with the output.

Of course, there are most likely going to be times when you would like to get an idea of how often the term does show up in the code or that part of the code. And in a few sections, we will show you how to make this happen. But for this part, you will only be able to pull up the word the first time that it is found by this method.

The Match Method

While there are some times when you will be able to work with the search method, and you will quickly see that there are a lot of things that it can do for your code, it isn't necessarily going to work with ever search and query that you would like to do. Another option that you can work with is the match method. This method is meant to help you find matches to the query, but they are only going to show up if that query item shows up at the beginning of your string. This method works well when you want it to find some specific patterns that may show up in the syntax that you would like to search through.

Looking at the example of code that we have above, you will be able to see how the match method is different compared to the search method. You can see that there is some pattern in that code, where the object of orange is going to show up between all of the words. But if you switch out the `re_search` for the re-match, then you are not going to get any results at all because orange is not the first term in that string.

Even though there is the object of orange found not only once, but twice, inside your code, it is not the first object that shows up in the string. The match method is just going to take a look at that first object that appears in the string. And since that is not going to be orange, then there is no match for you to see here.

Now, this is why it is so important to have your pattern in the right order right from the beginning. If the order is off, then you are not going to end up with the right answers here. You can change the pattern up any way that you would like when writing out the code. But once you get the code up and running, that pattern is going to stay put, and you aren't able to go through this and make any changes. With this example, with the patterns that we have is not going to have the orange show up first and with the match method, you will not get any result at all.

The Fidall Method

And the third method that we are going to work with here is going to be the final method. This is the option and search method that you will want to use when it is time to figure out how many instances of a particular object are found in a string. With the other methods that we have talked about, you are finding out if the object is found at all, or finding out if it is present as the first search item. But when you work with the final method, you are going to find out just how many oranges are present in that string. Using the code example that we had before, you are going to be able to replace it with the findall method and get the output of "orange, orange' since there are two oranges in the string.

Now, when you write out your code, you can have as many of the one object in the string as you would like. You could go through and have twenty oranges present in the string if you would like, and the findall is going to be able to put twenty oranges at the output. You can, of course, choose to work with a different object as well.

As you can see here, the findall method is a bit different compared to that search method that we talked about earlier in this chapter. Since they are a bit different, type the code into your compiler and experiment a bit with these three methods to see what outputs you can get with them as you make the necessary changes.

Working with these methods will make a big difference in the kind of searches that you can do with your code and the results that you can get with each one. Take some time to look through these and change up the code a bit to get some practice, and to see what each one can do for you.

Chapter 10: The Classes and the Objects in Python

Python is a language that is considered an OOP language, or an Object-Oriented Programming language. This may sound complicated, but it is going to mean that Python is designed in a way to make things much easier for the beginner to handle as they write their codes. The classes and the objects that are used for this language are set up to work together—ensuring that all of the information you write out in the code is going to stay where you put it and that everything maintains its organization.

To make things as simple as we can here, the classes that we will explore can be thought of as containers that are going to place all of the objects together inside. You can create as many of these containers as you would like, and then you go through and pick which objects will go into each class, based on what they have in common, and whether or not it makes sense for them to be in the same class or not. If the objects are found in the same class, then they are going to be pulled up at the same time when the code asks for them, helping to maintain the organization that we just talked about.

As a programmer working with the Python language, you will be able to make the objects that fit into an individual class what you would like, and there isn't a limit on how many objects can go into each class. With that in mind, you do need to make sure that the objects found in the same class are similar to one another. This makes your organization a bit easier and helps you to get the code to work a bit more efficiently for your needs.

Keep in mind here that just because the objects should be similar doesn't mean that they need to all be the same. However, if you or another programmer look at the classes, the objects that are inside should make sense, and they should be able to figure out how all of these objects are related.

The good thing here is that there are a lot of things that you will be able to do with these classes and these objects. But before we learn how to create some of our classes and place the objects that we want inside, we need to understand a few of the big differences between the classes and the objects. These key items include:

The objects that go into the same class need to have some similarities to one another. If someone looked into that class, it shouldn't be too hard for them to figure out how all of these items are related to each other. That doesn't mean that the items need to be identical, though. You could have a class that is labeled as fruits. You can then add in items like grapes, bananas, peaches, apples, and pears if you would like.

Classes: It is a good idea to learn about classes when you want to create a code in Python. Classes are the blueprint and the design for the objects because they will be there to tell the interpreter the right way to run your program.

Creating Your First Class

Now that we have a little bit of an understanding of what objects and classes are in the Python language, it is time to take this a step further and look at how you can create these classes. Despite how it may sound, this is a simple process to work with, as long as you make sure you are using the right syntax to put it all together.

To help you with creating your first class, you need to make sure that each class is getting a new definition created for it at the same time. When you are working on these classes, you need to have the keyword, and then right after that, you need to have the name that you want to give the class. Then, in the parentheses that follow, you need to have the superclass inside. Add in a colon at the end. Your program will still run if this part is missed out on, but it is considered good coding practices and makes it easier to read your code if you have that in there.

To help get rid of some of the confusion that can often happen with this syntax, we have a great example of how you would write out the code to create your Python class:

```python
class Vehicle(object):
#constructor
def_init_(self, steering, wheels, clutch, breaks, gears):
self._steering = steering
self._wheels = wheels
self._clutch = clutch
self._breaks =breaks
self._gears  = gears
#destructor
def_del_(self):
    print("This is destructor….")

#member functions or methods
def Display_Vehicle(self):
    print('Steering:' , self._steering)
    print('Wheels:', self._wheels)
    print('Clutch:', self._clutch)
    print('Breaks:', self._breaks)
    print('Gears:', self._gears)
#instantiate a vehicle option
myGenericVehicle = Vehicle('Power Steering', 4, 'Super Clutch', 'Disk Breaks', 5)
myGenericVehicle.Display_Vehicle()
```

The output that you are going to be able to get from putting all of this information into your interpreter includes:

```
('Steering:,' 'Power Steering')
('Wheels:,' 4)
('Clutch:'. 'Super Clutch')
('Breaks:,' 'Disk Breaks')
('Gears:,' 5)
```

To help you get some practice in writing out the classes that you want to use, take a few minutes to open up your compiler and type this in. As you can see with this example, there are a lot of parts that we need to look through. First, you see that there is a definition for the object. And then you see the attributes and the method definition.

IN addition to the above, there is going to be the class definition, the part of the code known as the destructor function, and then finally we are to the function. This is a lot of parts to keep track of, and it likely that you may not understand what is going on with each part, so let's break them all up and explore how they work and why they are so important to create your class in Python.

First, we have the object instantiation and class definition. These are both when it comes to the syntax of creating your class. This is because they are going to tell the code what needs to happen to get things done. The class definition is going to be the part of the code that we did above that says "`class subclass(superclass0)`", and then the part that comes with object instantiation is going to be the part that says "`object = class()`."

Then some special attributes come with this code. There are a few different special attributes that you can add to your code, depending on what you want to get done. Being able to understand what these attributes are all about will ensure that you can create a code the way that you want, and it also ensures that the interpreter knows what needs to happen in this part of the program. There are some special attributes that you can work within your code, but some of the most important ones—and the ones that you are going to use the most often as a beginner in Python include:

`__dict__` this is the direct variable of a class namespace

`__doc__` this is the document reference string of class

`__name__` this will be the class name

`__module__` this is the module name and consists of the class

`__bases__` this is the tuple that will also contain all of the superclasses

Memorizing these can help you out, but it may be nice to learn how they work inside of the code. Here is an example below that you can try out by typing into your compiler.

```
class Cat(object):
        itsWeight = 0
        itsAge = 0
        itsName = ""

        defMeow(self):
        print("Meow!")


        defDisplayCat(self):
        print("I    am    a    Cat    Object,    My    name    is",
self.itsName)
        print("My age is", self.itsAge)
        print("My weight is", self.itsWeight)

frisky = Cat()
frisky.itsAge = 10
frisky.itsName = "Frisky"
frisky.DisplayCat()
frisky.Meow()
```

When you are using this as your syntax in the interpreter, the result that you will get on the screen is:

```
('I am a Cat Object, My name is,' 'Frisky')
```

```
('My age is,' 10)
('My weight is,' 0)
Meow!
```

Once we are done with this part of the code, we are going to move onto the idea of accessing different members of your class. When you look through some of the different examples that we have done in this chapter, you may notice that we spent some time trying to identify our object, which, in this case, is `cat`, as being called Frisky. We were able to do that with the help of the dot operator.

This was helpful because it ensured that our program was able to access the members of the objects correctly. If you then look back at some of the code that we did before, you will notice that there are a fair number of variables that we can find inside of it. Sometimes, all of these variables may not make sense to use, especially since they are often inconvenient, and they are going to make a mess of the code that you are working with.

But there are times when you do need to have all of these variables present. How are you supposed to handle this and still make sure the code is going to work properly? You can use a few options to help you deal with this, without all of the issues. We are going to focus on the method that many programmers like to work with because it is easier to use. And this method is known as the accessor information. This is a good option because it helps you to get the information that you need without as much work.

You will find that it is straightforward to work with this method to help you take care of all those variables without a big mess. The syntax that works the best for ensuring that this can happen will include:

```
class Cat(object)
      itsAge = None
      itsWeight = None
      itsName = None
      #set accessor function use to assign values to
the fields or member vars
      def setItsAge(self, itsAge):
      self.itsAge = itsAge

      def setItsWeight(self, itsWeight):
      self.itsWeight = itsWeight

      def setItsName(self, itsName):
      self.itsName =itsName

      #get accessor function use to return the values
from a field
      def getItsAge(self):
      return self.itsAge
      def getItsWeight(self):
      return self.itsWeight
```

```
    def getItsName(self):
        return self.itsName

objFrisky = Cat()
objFrisky.setItsAge(5)
objFrisky.setItsWeight(10)
objFrisky.setItsName("Frisky")
print("Cats Name is:", objFrisky.getItsname())
print("Its age is:", objFrisky.getItsAge())
print("Its weight is:", objFrisky.getItsName())
```

The output that you are going to get from all of this will be the following:

```
('Cats Name is:', 'Frisky')
(Its age is:', 5)
('Its weight is:,' 10)
```

With the method that we just worked with above, we were able to place that accessor method and then we took a few steps to check whether or not it was able to work with the variables that we chose. This is going to be a good thing to work with because it helps us later during a few processes in Python, including data hiding and data encapsulation. When you want to make sure that the members who use the program can access the information, you will need to make sure that this method is open up to the public or some people will be blocked on it. But you also have the option of turning the viewing into either private or protected based on your own needs.

It is so important to know a bit about how the objects and classes in Python are going to work for you. If you can use them properly, these will not be all that complicated, but they will ensure that there is the right kind of organization of all the information in the code, ensuring that the program is going to run the way that you want. Take some time to practice a few of the codes that we have in this chapter to help you learn better how these classes work, and how you can use them on your projects.

Chapter 11: What Are the Operators and How Do You Use Them?

The next topic that we are going to explore in our Python codes are the operators. We have talked about these a bit throughout this guidebook, but now, we need to take a closer look at the way that they work, as well as why they can be so important to your success with writing. The good news is that these are pretty simple to work with, and it is likely that if you have done any coding so far, you have used a few of these operators already. However, since they can do some pretty amazing things with your code, it is worth our time to take a look at how to use them and all of the different things that they can do. Hence, with that introduction, let's take a closer look at how some of the operators are going to work when you are using Python.

Working with the Arithmetic Operator

The first type of operator that you will be able to use with your Python codes, and can be used regularly is the arithmetic operator. If you need to add together a few parts of your code, or you need to do some math inside of the code, then these operators are going to be the best ones for you to use. Whether you need to add, multiply, divide, or subtract, you will be able to use these operators to help you get the work done. The arithmetic operators that you are likely to use in Python include

(+): This sign is the operator for addition. Any time that you need to add together two parts of the code, you will use this operator.

(-): This is the sign for the operator of subtraction. Any time that you need to subtract two parts of your code, you are going to use this operator.

(*): This sign is the operator for multiplication. Any time that you would like to multiply together the two parts of a particular code, you would use this operator.

(/): This sign is the operator for dividing. Any time that you would like to divide two parts of the code, you can work with this operator.

When you are working in the Python language, you will be able to use any of these operators at any time that it is needed. You can even use more than one of these operators at the same time if it is needed. If you do bring in more than one type of the arithmetic operators in the same part of the code, you have to remember the order of operations. This means that you will handle the multiplier operators first, and then you go to the division, making sure you go from the left side to the right side. Once those are done, you can do all of the addition operators and end with the subtraction operators, going from left to right as well.

Working with the Comparison Operators

In addition to using the arithmetic operators, you can also work inside your code with the comparison operator. These comparison operators are a great option to work with any time that you have two or more values or statements that show up in the code, and you are looking to compare them or bring them together.

It is common to see these when you are working with Boolean expressions because they need to work from the idea of the statements, either being the same or being different, which is true or false. You will either have it that the statements or the numbers you are working within the code end up being the same, or they are not the same. This is how we come to working with the Boolean expressions. Some of the different operators that fit in this category in the Python language include:

(>=): this one means to check if the left-hand operand is greater than or equal to the value of the one on the right.

(<=) : this one means to check if the value of the left-hand operand is less than or equal to the one on the right.

(>) : this one means to check whether the values of the left side are greater than the value on the right side of the code.

(<) : this one means to check whether the values of the left side are less than the values that are on the right side.

(!=) : this is the "not equal to" operator.

(==) : this one is the "equal to" operator.

As you go through this and work on the program or the code, you may find that you have already started to use this kind of operator in some of the codes that we already have, and you haven't even realized it yet! You can easily set up some conditions inside of the code, and when you do this, you want to make sure that the code will meet these conditions before it continues. This is where the comparison operators are going to come in and be helpful.

With this idea, you will have your comparison in place, and then the user can come on and put in the information they want. The comparison operator is then going to take a look at that input, and compare it against the conditions that you set. This allows the program to figure out if the input and the condition you set are the same or different from each other. This can help you get more out of the program and ensures that you get the right results with your program.

Working with the Logical Operators

The third type of operators that you can work within Python will be the logical operators. These are a good kind of operator to work with because they can take the input that the user gives to them, and then evaluate that information based on the conditions that the programmer put into that code. There are a few types of operators that are going to fit into this idea, but the three common ones, and the ones that a beginner is most likely to use for their programs, will include:

Or: This is the logical operator that will have the compiler is going to value "x," and if it is false, then it is going to move on and evaluate y. If it notices that x is true, then the compiler is going to return the evaluation of x to the user.

And: With this one, if x is the false answer, then the compiler will stop and evaluate that statement or that part of the code. But if x ends up being the true part, it will skip that part of the code, and move on to evaluating y.

Not: If the compiler looks at x and finds that it is false, then the compiler is going to return the result of True. On the other hand, if x is true, then the program is going to return False as the answer.

As you can see, these logical operators are pretty similar to what we saw with the comparison operators. But you will find that these kinds of operators are going to work a bit differently. You will only need to work with these types of operators when you need to use the specific situations that we listed above, and not for every situation.

Working with the Assignment Operators

The final operator type that you can work within Python is the assignment operator. This one is going to use the equal sign to take one or more values (usually it is one with beginner programming, but can easily be more if you choose), over to any variable that you are working with. So, if you would like to take your chosen variable and assign 100 to it as the value, you will need to put an equal sign between the two of these to show that the value is assigned to that variable in the code.

There are going to be some times when you will write out a particular code and will need to use the assignment operator, using it in the code so that it knows what value is assigned to the variable. If you look through some of the different codes that we have worked on throughout this guidebook, there are various examples of how the assignment operator can use. Any time that you would like to talk with the compiler and have it assign a value to the variable, then this assignment operator is what you need to use so that the compiler knows what value is there.

As we briefly mentioned, it is possible to take more than one value and assign it to the variable that you would use. Doing this is easier than it may seem, as long as you make sure to list it all out in the proper manner to get this to work for you. You need to have the right signs in place and make sure that you put the equal sign in between the values that are meant to go with that chosen variable. You don't have to limit yourself to just two or three values to the variable if you want to expand this out more. It is possible to assign as many values to the same variable if you would like.

Of course, the more values that you try to assign to the same variable, the more complicated the code is going to get. As a beginner, it is often best to stick with the codes that will just put one or two values to each variable, and then work up to some of the more complicated things as you go. This is going to make the process of writing out code a lot easier, and you won't have to worry about where the signs go and whether or not the compiler is going to understand what you are doing.

Because this is a very common operator to work with and it has a lot of power behind it, it is important that you learn how to use this kind of operator. There are a lot of times when you are going to have a variable in your code, and it is going to be useless if you don't assign some value to it. This value is going to make sure that the compiler can call up the variable, and that it is going to be usable in the code that you are writing. But if you don't know how to work with the assignment operator, then putting value back to the variable is going to become impossible.

As you can see, these operators, in all of their different forms, are going to be important parts of the code that you are working on. The ones that we have gone through above for this chapter are some of the most common operators that you can work with, and they are going to make it easier for you to do some neat things in your code.

You can use these operators to add in some more power, to compare some of the information that you want to use in your code, and adding them will be easy. You just need to look through the different types of code that we have gone through in this guidebook, and all of the examples and even though they are seen as basic codes to help you get more familiar with this coding language, they are still going to contain a lot of the different operators that we just talked about. No matter what kind of code you decide to work with, you are going to find a lot of use when you learn how to work with these operators.

Chapter 12: The Variables in the Python Language

We have spent a lot of different topics inside this guidebook so far. We have looked at how to work with inheritances, how to make our exceptions inside a code, how to create our loops, and so much more. Now, we need to take a look at the next topic of variables and how they are going to work in the Python code.

To keep this process simple, the variables are going to be anything inside the code that can hold onto a value that may or may not change. The variable is just like a box that can hold onto things, mainly information in this case. And they are essential for a programmer to work with, in Python and other coding languages, because these variables will ensure that when the code runs, the compiler is going to be able to pull out the right value at the right time.

These variables are just going to be like a stored into the memory of your computer and in the code. You will then be able to tell the compiler that you want these variables to be pulled out when it is time. This means that the variables that you go and write into the code are stored and found on a specific location in the memory of your computer. If they were not stored in that specific point, then it would be hard for the compiler to bring these back up when you were running the code.

You want to make sure that the variables are given the right value as you work through this kind of code. It makes it easier for you to pull up the values that are assigned to it at a later point. Depending on the data you want to put into the code, the variable can save the right space in the memory of your computer and makes it easier to find it later on.

How Do I Assign a Value Over to the Variable?

Before the variable can do the job that it needs to, it has to have at least one value that is assigned to it. Otherwise, it is just an empty box found on the memory of the computer, with nothing in it. It isn't going to pull up anything on the computer when the program decides to go through and run the program. If the variable as a value assigned to it the way that it should (and at times, you will want to have more than one value assigned back to the same variable), then it is more likely to react the way you are looking for with your code as long as you did everything else right in the code.

As you get more familiar with working on these variables, you will find that these come in three different options that you can use. Each of them is going to be brought up in different situations based on the code that you want to write, and the type of value that you decide to assign to that variable. Some of the main choices that you will get to work with when it comes to variable types include:

Float: this would include numbers like 3.14 and so on.
String: this is going to be like a statement where you could write out something like "Thank you for visiting my page!" or another similar phrase.
Whole number: this would be any of the other numbers that you would use that do not have a decimal point.

When you decide to work with some variables in your code, you must remember that you won't have to take the time to make any declarations before a spot in the memory is saved for you. This is something that automatically happens once you use the equal sign and get the value assigned over to the variable as we talked about in the operators. If you want to double check and see if this is what is going to happen when you run the code, look to see if there is an equal sign that appears before the value or values and the variable that they are assigned to.

The process of assigning a value or values over to your chosen variable is going to be a simple process to work with. You need to work with the equal sign between the two of these to make it work. A couple of good examples of how you can do this will include:

```
x = 12              #this  is  an  example  of  an  integer
assignment
pi = 3.14    #this  is  an  example  of  a  floating  point
assignment
customer name = John Doe      #this  is  an  example  of  a
string assignment
```

Another option that you can do here, and that we have mentioned a little bit in this chapter already is to have a variable assigned to two or more values. There are some instances when you are writing code, and you will need to take two values and place them with the same variable.

To do this, you need to use the same procedure that we talked about above. Just make sure that you add in an equal sign to each part to help the compiler know that these are all associated with the same variable. So, you would want to write out something like a = b = c = 1 to show the compiler that each of these variables equals one. Or you could have 1 = b = 2 to show that there are two values to a variable.

The most important thing to remember here is that the variable needs to be assigned to a value to work in the code and that these variables are simply spots that are reserved in the memory for those values. Then, when the compiler needs to call up those values, it simply will call up the variable to bring everything out.

As you can see, working with variables can be a simple process, but it is still something that you should spend some time with. There are a lot of different things that you can save in a variable, and assigning the right value or values over to your variable will ensure that the compiler can bring them up and provides you with the results that you need. Make sure to practice assigning a value over to the variable of your choice, and even assigning multiple values over to the variable of your choice so that you can get more familiar with how all of this works.

Chapter 13: Troubleshooting a Python Program When Things Aren't Working as Planned

As a beginner, the idea of writing out a whole coding language can sometimes seem like a big deal and something overwhelming to work with. We took a lot of time to look at the different parts of the code that you can work with and explored some examples to help you see what works and what might not work in your code.

As you are starting to learn more about Python coding and all of the different parts that come with it, you may run into some troubles that you are going to need to deal with. Maybe your program isn't working the way that you think it should, and you keep getting an error message that shouldn't be there—or perhaps you don't know how to fix the problem when you do run into this issue. The good news is there are some simple things that even a beginner can do with their program to get it up and running and to ensure that they are going to be able to get back to coding sooner. Some of the best troubleshooting ideas that you can work within Python include:

Print Out the Code Often

It is never a good idea to write out hours of code, and then go and test it. This may work if you get everything right. But if you get something wrong, you now need to go back through and fix all of the things that you did wrong. And that is a lot of code to go through and look for errors. Printing the information out and testing the code regularly will ensure that you aren't going to run into this problem.

This doesn't mean that you have to print out after each line. But it does mean to print often. If you can print out after each small bit of code, this will make it easier when things aren't working the way that you want. If you have been printing out the information after every five minutes of coding for example, and all of a sudden something in the code isn't working, you know exactly where the mistake is, and you won't have to go through and search through all of the pages and all of the coding again.

Start with Some of the Codes You Already Know

As a beginner, there is a lot of new stuff that you are going to need to focus on to ensure that you get the results that you want out of your project. But thanks to the information in this guidebook, you now know how to work on some of the basics of the code in Python. When you are in doubt about some of the things that you need to do in different situations, then it is a good idea to do some practice with existing code, and codes that you know work already.

Many beginners find that it is better for them to start with some structures and syntaxes that are in existence already, and then you can go through and make the small changes that are needed for your code. This ensures that the code is going to work, and can save some headaches along the way. As you use these existing code structures and learn how they work a bit more, you will then be able to write them on your own. But in the beginning, this is a good way to get started and see the results that you want.

When you are ready to work on a project on your own, then there are a lot of resources that you can use to help you find the code that you want to work with. A quick Google search is going to be able to help you find the structure of the code that you need. It doesn't have to be what you will need for that project exactly, but having the basic syntax is going to make things easier and will help you to get the code started. From there, you can make the changes that you want and then check out the code to make sure that all of the implanted changes are the ones that you want.

After Small Changes, Run the Code to Check It Out

Do not start with a blank file, sit down, and spend an hour coding before you even try out the code for the first time. You will make the work harder for yourself, and when there are a whole bunch of little errors that pop up, you won't know where to start. It can take forever to go through it all and fix whatever is going wrong.

Instead, every few minutes, you should run the updates and test the code to see if something comes up. That way, when a bug does show up in the code, you only have a few lines or so of the code to check for the issue rather than a whole bunch of code. It isn't possible for you to test out your code too often, so do it as much as you can.

Always remember that the more code that you write before you test it again, the more places where errors can occur and the more code that you will need to search through again. And each time that you do go through and run the code, you will get some more feedback on your work so you can learn as you go.

This may seem like it is slowing down your coding skills and what you can do to get the code done, but in reality, it is going to make a difference for what you can get done, and the amount of time that you will spend on each project. If you have to go through and have to change the information on two hours of work, then this is going to take longer to find the mistake than it is worth. If you have to go through and heck a small block of code at a time, then you will be able to find the error faster and get back on to your coding.

Take the Time to Read Any Error Messages

If you do make a mistake in some of the codes that you are writing, you are going to see an error message show up. When this does happen, you should read through the description, because this can point out what is wrong with your code and how you can fix it. Let's say that you get an error message that says that the language runtime tried to execute the program but ran into a problem. What this means is that you skipped on a step in your code writing, or there was a typo, or something else is missing from the code. You will know what to fix from this information and can get int here and make sure it is done.

If you are first getting started with Python programming, then it is possible that a message will come up and you won't understand what it is saying. But you should still read through it and see what information is there. At a minimum, you will at least get a line number on this message, and you can take a look on that line of your code to see what is going on.

For those who have tried the other steps and still are not able to figure out what the error message is all about, then you do have the option of going online and searching for it. Some error messages can be confusing, and even if you go back through the lines and try to check, you may not be able to find the error and how to fix it.

Doing an online search can help tell you exactly what is going on. You can copy and paste the last line of that error message into Google and see what comes up. There will likely be at least a few results when you type this in as other coders were probably met with this message and had questions as well. This should provide you with some information on what is wrong in the code, and you can go back through and figure out what is wrong with your code and fix it all up.

Even though this is a great way to get answers to the questions that you have, especially when you are not able to figure out what the error message means—but don't just run to this for every time that an error message shows up. You aren't going to learn much about coding and how to fix your own mistakes if you are just relying on Google to answer all of your questions.

Try to take a look at the error and look through the code to see if you can fix it on your own. And then, if you get stuck, utilize this option for your own needs.

Guess on the Fix and Then Check It Out

If you try a few of the other methods and still aren't sure about how to fix something, you may need to try out a few different things to see what is going to happen. You should already be running your code as often as possible to provide you with some quick feedback. Keep doing this as you try out a few options and see whether it fixes your error or not.

There is a possibility that the fix you are trying is going to introduce a new error, and sometimes it can be hard to tell if you are nearing a solution or making things worse. Try not to do this for so long that you have no idea how to get back to your starting position.

Trying out a few different things can be important because it helps you to learn more about your code and then if you do ask someone else for help, they are going to ask you what you have tried already. They probably will be more annoyed than anything if they hear that you haven't tried anything, but if you list out a few things that you already tried, then they know where to start from that place.

Use the Process of Commenting Out the Code

No matter what kind of coding language you decide to work with, there is going to be the option to comment in your work. This is a way that you can leave a little note or some information in the code, but in a way that ensures that the compiler isn't going to try and execute that note in the program. This can be an advantage for you as you write the code because you will also be able to use it to help troubleshoot the issues in your project.

If you are writing some code and find that you keep getting an error message, but nothing that you are doing seems to work to fix it, then you may want to comment out the code. You can pick a part of the code that you think is causing the issue, and then just at the # sign to the front of it. This takes it out of the code basically, without erasing all of it.

If the script that you are working on is pretty long, then you can go through here and comment out some of the parts of the code, specifically the parts that aren't going to have a direct relation to the changes that you plan to work on. This is going to help because you will be able to search through just the code that has the mistake, and it speeds up the whole process.

Be careful when you are doing the commenting out process; you do need to be a bit careful. It isn't going to help you too much if you end up commenting out the parts that are needed to set the variables. If you do this, then the program is going to stop working, and you will end up with a mess trying to get the program to run. Start by commenting out just small parts of the code first and add on as you need to do more testing. It ensures that you don't eliminate some parts of the code that you need at that time.

After you have finished using the "commenting out" method to help you test your code, and you are sure that it is ready to go without the error, then it is time to go back through the code and remove any comment characters that you put there. This takes some time, but it will help you to turn the whole program on so that it runs the application that you were writing.

Ask Someone for Help If It Is Needed

At some point, you may have tried the troubleshooting options that we have listed above, and maybe even a few others of your own, and you are still not able to get the code to behave in the manner that you would like. If you have done all of that and still see an error message that you are not able to fix yet, then it is time to see if there is someone else out there who you can ask for help.

Every programmer needs help at some point or another, and there is nothing wrong with asking and receiving help when you get stuck. If you do ask for help (hopefully after taking a small break from doing the coding to ensure that you are not overworking yourself and missing some big things that you could fix), you need to have the following things in place and ready to answer so that the other person knows how to help you out exactly:

Explain what you want the program to do for you and where the error is occurring.

Show the other person the code that is sending you an error so they can see it for themselves.

Show the other person the stack trace, all of it, including the message you got stating the error.

Explain everything that you have already tried on the error. This helps the other person have a good idea of what you have tried, and what they should try to get the code to work.

Working on a Python code can be a rewarding experience. There are a lot of benefits to working with this code—and as you can see from the examples in this guidebook, as well as some of the troubleshooting that we just looked at, there are also a lot of neat codes and other programs that you can write, even as a beginner!

Conclusion

Thank you for making it through to the end of *Python Programming*! Let's hope it was informative and able to provide you with all of the tools you need to achieve your goals—whatever they may be.

The next step is to get started with writing some of your codes using the great Python coding language to help you out. This guidebook gave you all of the tools that you need to get started with this kind of language. We explored what the Python language is all about, along with many of the benefits that seem to draw programmers in, whether they are beginners or not, and entices them to get started with this language. We even looked at the steps that you need to take to start installing this program on your computer, no matter what kind of operating system you are using.

Writing a new coding language can sometimes seem complicated. You may worry that the text and all of the little parts of it are going to be too complicated for you to figure out on your own—and this is what keeps a lot of people away from trying out this code, in the first place. However, when it comes to working with a particular code in this language, all of those fears can be put to rest. As you saw throughout this guidebook and the many codes that we explored, writing out a particular code in this language is easy and fun to do! Even as a beginner, you are going to catch on quickly.

This guidebook is full of all the different codes, syntaxes, and information that you need to get started with writing some of your codes. We not only took a look at how to install this program on your computer—but we also broke down how to work with many of the common things that show up in this language. Whether your coding will require you to work with exceptions, loops, conditional statements, regular expressions, inheritances, or a combination of them all (and some of the other topics that we discussed in this guidebook), you now know exactly how to use them to your advantage when you write out some of your codes.

There are so many benefits that can come from working on a Python code for your reasons. Beginners love this language for so many reasons—and now that you know a bit more about it and how all of the different parts of the code work together, you can easily see why they are even more advanced coders are drawn to this language for some of their projects. It is incredible how something easy to use can be so powerful, and have so much diversity and options to go with it. When you are ready to learn more about the Python coding language and try out some of the different codes that we talked about, then make sure to check out this guidebook, and use it to get started!

www.ingramcontent.com/pod-product-compliance
Lightning Source LLC
Chambersburg PA
CBHW070350220526
45467CB00001B/327